amsale aberra
fashion designer

Born in Ethiopia but separated from her parents in the 1970s during a time of political chaos, Amsale Aberra came to the US to study art, then political science, and finally fashion design.

After she finished her schooling, Aberra landed a job at a fashionable New York clothing company, and in 1985 she and her partner decided to marry. But looking through the glossy bridal magazines of the time, Aberra could find nothing that matched her simple, clean style.

Wedding gowns at the time were lavish, lacy, sequined, poufy, and over-the-top. So Aberra decided to design and sew her own dress. Then she started making custom dresses for other brides who shared her taste.

Her designs became so popular that she opened her own studio. She sold high-priced evening and wedding gowns to wealthy people around the world, but she also designed a more affordable line of wedding gowns.

Celebrities like Vanessa Williams, Katy Perry, and Halle Berry have worn Aberra's gowns, and her clothes have appeared in movies and television shows.

Aberra's last runway show came at her request in April 2018, a few weeks after she sadly died from uterine cancer.

1954-2018

stacey abrams
politician - author - attorney

Stacey Abrams is the first African-American woman ever to be a major political party candidate for governor in Georgia.

When she ran for the office as a Democrat in 2018, Georgia had had 82 previous governors in a row who were men.

Her Republican opponent, Brian Kemp, barely squeaked out the 50 percent of votes he needed to avoid a runoff election with Abrams.

It was the closest gubernatorial election in Georgia since 1966, and Abrams has gone on to be one of the most important voices in the Democratic party and a leader of its get-out-the-vote efforts in Georgia.

Before turning to politics, Abrams was an accomplished lawyer who worked for a respected law firm and then the city of Atlanta. She also wrote romance novels under a pen name and ran a consulting business.

Abrams was elected to the Georgia House of Representatives in 2006. In 2018, her book, Minority Leader: How to Lead from the Outside and Make Real Change, was published.

1973-

claudia alexander
space scientist - author

Fascinated by the idea of other worlds, Claudia Alexander became an important researcher at NASA, the National Aeronautics and Space Administration.

As a young girl in a nearly all-white school, Alexander struggled with feelings of loneliness, but as a grown-up she built bridges with other countries.

Alexander was the US representative to the Rosetta Project, an international effort to study comets.

She was also the last project manager for the US's Galileo mission to Jupiter, which launched in 1989 and ended in 2003. The project surprised Alexander by showing that the moons of Jupiter were not like she expected. Alexander saw the discovery as an exciting learning experience.

Alexander shared her love of scientific exploration in a series of children's' books and by mentoring children, especially African-American girls.

Sadly, Alexander died of breast cancer in 2015, ten years after her diagnosis.

1959-2015

danielle allen
professor - author

Danielle Allen's junior year of college was a turning point for her. That was when she learned about income inequality in America.

During her own life, Allen felt that she had not suffered much racial discrimination, and it was only after learning the statistics on income equality that she came to understand some of the country's racial injustices.

After graduating from Princeton University and earning a doctoral degree from Oxford, Allen became a professor at the University of Chicago. She saw first-hand the poverty and violence of the neighborhoods surrounding the campus.

This inspired her to create the Civic Knowledge Project to increase communication between the University and the outside community. She taught night classes to help provide opportunities for working adults.

Allen also published books looking at the Brown v. Board of Education decision and the US Constitution, arguing for the importance of creating mutual trust between different social groups in the fight for political equality for all.

1971-

maya angelou
writer - activist - performer

Maya Angelou lived a colorful life, one filled with pain but also beauty.

Her renowned autobiographical works testify to what it was like to grow up Black and female in the United States, both in the rural segregated South and in more northern urban areas.

Angelou's story begins in I Know Why the Caged Bird Sings and continues in 5 more volumes.

The books tell of Angelou's struggles as a 17-year-old single mother and her career as a singer, dancer and actress in the 1950s. Her performance in a production of Porgy and Bess inspired her to take a more active role in raising awareness of the social history of Black people.

Leaving behind her career as a performer, Angelou joined the Harlem Writers Guild and became the northern coordinator for Martin Luther King Jr.'s new civil rights organization.

In the years that followed, Angelou continued to write and travel, and she resumed work as an actor. She wrote poems, speeches, and nonfiction and was widely honored for many of her works and performances. In 2011, President Barack Obama awarded Angelou the Presidential Medal of Freedom.

1928-2014

gladys bentley
jazz & blues singer

Gladys Bentley didn't let the world tell her who to be.

From childhood, Bentley knew that the traditional female gender roles she was taught weren't right for her. She began wearing her brother's clothes and, when her parents refused to accept her, ran away to Harlem at age 16. There she began a successful career as a jazz and blues singer and activist.

Bentley became one of the first openly homosexual headliners in mainstream New York City clubs - even as she continued wearing traditionally male attire, including tails and a top hat. Her act became very popular and she bought an apartment on Fifth Avenue.

In the 1920s, she was signed to the record label Okeh, which was one of the earliest labels to produce African-American music. Censorship of her often-colorful club lyrics, though, seems to have limited the audience for her records.

She married a white woman in a civil ceremony in 1931. In later years, under increasing pressure to conform to society"s expectations, Bentley claimed to have been cured of her attraction to women. Whether Bentley believed this or not remains a mystery.

1907-1960

halle berry
actor

Halle Berry made her motion picture debut in Spike Lee's 1991 movie Jungle Fever. She quickly became one of the most sought after A-list stars in Hollywood.

Berry has taken on a wide variety of roles, including action hero, African queen, and drug addict.

In 2002, Berry received the Academy Award for her performance in the film Monster's Ball, which tells the story of a complicated interracial relationship between a Black woman played by Berry and a racist white man.

Berry's personal life, though, has had its challenges. Her father was Black and her mother was white, and Berry described feeling unwanted because of her race in the mostly-white school she attended starting at age 10.

Berry's difficult relationships with men were often topics in the tabloid press, including her charges of abuse against one partner and a public custody dispute with an ex-husband.

Berry continues today to act in a range of film and TV roles. Besides the Academy Award, she has won Emmy, Golden Globe, Screen Actors Guild, and many other awards.

1966–

beyoncé
singer - actor - entrepreneur

Even as a child, Beyoncé Knowles knew she was born to be a performer.

When she was 8 years old, she beat out dozens of other girls for a spot in a new singing group, Girl's Tyme, and with the group she performed on the TV show Star Search.

Losing the competition didn't make Beyoncé give up her dreams. Her father took over the group's management and, after the group changed names and members several times, the four-member Destiny's Child was born. In 1995, the group signed its first record deal, while Beyonce was still in high school.

Beyoncé became a breakout star when Destiny's Child's second album sold 10 million copies, had a long string of hit songs, and won two Grammy awards.

In the years after, Beyonce went on to a hugely successful solo career as a singer, actor, and entrepreneur.

She has contributed time and money to many causes, including opening a cosmetology training school for drug rehabilitation residents, supporting Michelle Obama's childhood anti-obesity campaign, and supporting victims of Gulf Coast hurricanes.

1981-

london breed
politician

In June 2018 London Breed became the first Black woman to serve as mayor of San Francisco, California.

As mayor, Breed has shown her strong commitment to addressing the city's affordable housing crisis.

Breed herself grew up in a public housing project in a poor and violent section of Los Angeles. She watched as her siblings became drug addicts. Her sister tragically overdosed, and her brother was sent to prison for robbery.

Breed, however, managed not only to graduate high school but to go on to college and graduate school.

She earned a master of public administration degree and started a career in public service.

She worked in the Office of Housing and Neighborhood Services, then was appointed director of the African-American Art and Culture Complex. Breed was elected to the San Francisco Board of Supervisors, where she made it her mission to fight for tenants' rights and housing security. Breed was forced to leave her position at the Board of Supervisors when she was elected mayor in 2018 but carries on her cause.

1974-

paulette brown
lawyer

In 2015, Paulette Brown became the first woman of color to serve as President of the American Bar Association. During her time in service, Brown spearheaded several diversity initiatives.

Calling out the striking lack of diversity in the practice of law, Brown has long tried to promote diversity and inclusion in the profession and to enhance her colleagues' understanding of cultural differences.

A graduate of Howard University and Seton Hall, Brown has had a distinguished career as an attorney. She worked for many years as the in-house counsel for Fortune 500 companies before becoming a law firm partner.

Brown has been named one of the Best Lawyers in America numerous times by US News. She was in the Ebony Power 100 List in 2014, and the National Law Journal recognized her as one of the 50 Most Influential Minority Lawyers in America. Savoy Magazine has named her one of the Most Influential Black Lawyers.

1951-

ursula burns
business executive, engineer

Ursula Burns is the first African-American woman to serve as a CEO in a Fortune 500 company. The position came as the peak of a long career at Xerox.

As a child, she lived with her single mother and two siblings in a low-income project in New York City. She earned her bachelor's degree and then took part in a graduate engineering program for minorities where Xerox helped pay for her education in mechanical engineering at Columbia University.

Burns started as an intern at the company, then was hired as engineer. Over the years, she worked her way up to various managerial positions. She was known for her innovative thinking and openness to new ideas.

Between 2009 and 2016, Burns led the White House's STEM (science, technology, engineering, and mathematics) program. (STEM) In 2010, Burns was named Export Council vice chair under President Barack Obama. In 2016, she was on Hillary Clinton's list of potential vice-presidential running mates.

1958–

cheryl contee
blogger - social media guru

Cheryl Contee co-founded the influential blog Jack and Jill Politics in 2006 to offer a view of American politics from a middle-class Black perspective.

Contee writes for the blog under the pseudonym Jill Tubman, with Baratunde Thurston writing as Jack Turner. The blog was established to combat the media's stereotyping of Black people as either criminals or mega-elites. It gives a voice to diverse ideas and viewpoints from within the Black community.

Contee also co-founded Fission Strategy, a social media consulting company that helps non-profits that want to better society. Fission helps connects these organizations to their supporters.

1971-

dorothy cotton
civil rights activist

Dorothy Cotton was an important leader in the civil rights movement of the 1960s.

She worked under Martin Luther King, Jr. in the Southern Christian Leadership Conference (SCLC). As leader of its Citizenship Education Program, Cotton worked to inspire African-Americans to register to vote and to organize in their communities. Cotton continued to advocate for social change, human rights, and Black leadership for most of her life.

Cotton grew up in the 1930s in a three-room shack in North Carolina with her father, a tobacco worker, and three sisters. She credits her high school English and drama teacher for helping her apply to college and get three part-time jobs to support her studies.

Cotton became actively involved in the Civil Rights movement from the very start. She helped organize the mass protests in Birmingham, Alabama, in 1963 and took part in numerous anti-segregationist activities starting in 1964.

In 2012, Cotton published a book called If Your Back's Not Bent: The Role of the Citizenship Education Program in the Civil Rights Movement.

1930-2018

cheryl mckissack daniel

engineer, business executive

Cheryl McKissack Daniel runs the United States' oldest minority-owned construction company, McKissack and McKissack, founded in 1905. The firm has also been entirely female-owned since 1988.

Daniel's grandfather and great-uncle, who started the company, were the first two Black licensed architects in America. The company has been passed down through the family in different forms ever since. Engineering and design, it seems, is in the McKissack family's blood.

In their youth, the three McKissack sisters - Andrea and twins Cheryl and Deryl - often spent Saturdays with their father at the office, learning to trace and shade his architectural drawings. Afterward, they'd eat lunch and put on hard hats to go to see some job sites.

All three of the girls went on to study construction and design-related fields in college. Daniel worked as an engineer for NASA and the US Department of Defense until her father's death, when she returned home to New York and struck out on her own, forming the McKissack Group.

When her mother decided to step down from McKissack and McKissack, Cheryl McKissack Daniel bought it from her, managed a reorganization, and took on leadership of the firm, which now earns about $50 million in revenue per year. Meanwhile, her sister Deryl runs a separate, more design-focused McKissack and McKissack in Washington, DC.

1961-

julie dash
filmmaker

Julie Dash wrote and directed the first feature film by an African-American woman to receive a nationwide US theatrical release.

The 1991 film, Daughters of the Dust, tells the story of three generations of descendants of slaves. The family lives on St. Helena Island, off the coast of South Carolina and Georgia, but are preparing to migrate to the North. Their ancestors were brought to the island centuries earlier, and over time they developed a creole language known as Gullah or Sea Island Creole English. The story is influenced by Dash's own heritage and prominently features women characters who challenge Hollywood stereotypes of Black women.

The film was critically acclaimed, successful at the box office, and recognized with an award for best cinematography at the Sundance Film Festival. Yet Dash was the only prize winner there who was not offered a film deal prior to leaving the Festival. Many believe Dash suffers exclusion from the industry because she is Black and a woman.

In the years since Daughters of the Dust, Dash has continued filming but has turned to music videos, commercials, TV movies, and documentaries.

helen octavia dickens
physician - educator

Helen Octavia Dickens was the daughter of a former slave who went on to accomplish remarkable things.

Her father, who was a nine-year-old slave when the Civil War ended, encouraged his daughter to pursue a career in medicine. Dickens went on to become the first Black woman to be Board certified in gynecology and obstetrics in Philadelphia. In 1956, she became the first Black woman to join the faculty of University of Pennsylvania's School of Medicine.

There, Dickens created one of the earliest US teen pregnancy clinics and recruited minority students to medicine at the University.

Dickens published studies of teen pregnancy throughout her career and received many awards for her teaching, counseling, advocacy for women, and work on uterine cancer.

1909-2001

noma dumezweni

actor

Noma Dumezweni's father fought against apartheid - forced racial segregation - in Africa. The family eventually fled and became refugees. When Dumezweni was 7, her mother settled herself and her two daughters in England.

Dumezweni went on to become an acclaimed actor, winning the Olivier Award (similar to the US's Tony Awards) in 2006 for her role in the play A Raisin in the Sun.

Dumezweni became an international star when she was cast as the adult Hermione in the 2006 stage play Harry Potter and the Cursed Child.

But her performance also generated controversy because of the color of her skin. A white actor had played the character in all of the Harry Potter movies. JK Rowling, author of the Harry Potter books, defended the choice of Dumezweni for the role. Rowling noted that she had never stated the color of Hermione's skin at all.

Dumezweni went on to win a second Olivier Award for that role in 2016, and she performed her part on Broadway beginning in 2018 and continuing until March 2020, when the COVID-19 pandemic shut down the theaters.

Over her career, Dumezweni has performed a variety of roles on the stage, in film, and on television.

1969-

erica garner
activist

Erica Garner was an activist who fought against police brutality.

The issue was very personal for Garner, whose father Eric died when New York City police placed him in a choke hold. Eric Garner was supposedly selling cigarettes illegally on the streets. His final words - "I can't breathe!" - became a rallying cry for Black Americans and a symbol of their experiences with law enforcement.

Erica Garner led the charge, calling for police accountability, leading Black Lives Matter marches, and speaking to the media about law enforcement, racial biases, and the mistreatment of communities of color.

Garner led peaceful protests every week for a year after her father's death, spoke out on social media to raise awareness of unfair policing practices, and formed the Garner Way Foundation.

Tragically, Garner died in 2017 from a heart attack triggered by asthma and an enlarged heart.

1990-2017

whoopi goldberg
comedian - activist - actor

Whoopi Goldberg's life has been one of highs and lows. She loved acting even as a child and starred in stage plays starting at age 8.

In high school, though, she started taking drugs and became an addict. Finally, she sought help, cleaned up, married her counselor, and had a child while still in her teens - then quickly divorced.

Goldberg next set off for California to rekindle her dream of performing and started doing stand up and sketch comedy. Goldberg offered social commentary through the characters she played, including a drug addict with a Ph.D. and a young Black girl who bathes in bleach and dreams of becoming white. Her talent was recognized, and she was given a Broadway show.

Goldberg's career took off quickly, and she played high-profile roles in the film The Color Purple and in Comic Relief, a benefit raising money for the homeless. Goldberg has fought for environmental causes, against hunger, and for drug abuse and AIDS awareness.

Goldberg's brash and outspoken style sometimes kept her from getting roles or recognition as a performer, but she has shown that she will not be silenced, and she always seems to bounce back.

1955-

kamala harris
politician - attorney

Kamala Harris is the first woman of color to run for Vice President on a major-party ticket - and the first to win.

Throughout her career in law and politics, Harris has worked within the country's existing institutions to try to bring positive change for minorities and the disadvantaged.

The daughter of an Indian-born mother and Jamaican-born father, Harris graduated from Howard University and earned her law degree.

She worked as a prosecutor in California. Harris was the first Black woman and the first southeast-Asian woman to be elected District Attorney for San Francisco county - and, later, California Attorney General. Not everyone agreed with her policies, but she is widely praised for her San Francisco Back on Track initiative, which offered young, first-time offenders an alternative to prison time.

In 2016, she was elected the second Black woman ever to serve in the US Senate. When male Senators tried to silence her, Harris refused to be quiet.

Harris ran for US President during the Democratic primaries in 2020. When Joe Biden, Jr. received the nomination, he invited Harris to run as Vice President. They won the election.

1964-

jahana hayes
educator - politician

2016's National Teacher of the Year Jahana Hayes has learned some of life's lessons the hard way.

Her mother was addicted to drugs, and as a child Hayes lived with her grandmother in public housing - and at times homeless. At 17, Hayes became a single mother, but with the encouragement of her teachers, she held onto her dream of a college education.

Years later, she earned a bachelor's degree and was certified to teach history. She went on to earn advanced degrees in education. She went to work in the same high school she had attended.

After receiving the 2016 National Teacher of the Year Award and meeting President Barack Obama, Hayes realized she was a role model for her students, whose own lives were like hers had been. She decided she wanted to show her students not to hold back on their dreams and ran for Congress.

Hayes became the first Black Democrat ever to represent Connecticut in Congress in 2019.

1973-

michelle howard
naval officer

Michelle Howard was one of only seven women in her Naval Academy class of over 1,300. Women had not even been allowed to enroll in the Naval Academy until two years earlier.

Howard's distinguished career after her graduation has shown how much women naval officers can achieve.

She was honored for her leadership skills early on, and she served for a time as the liaison to the Defense Advisory Committee on Women in the Military Service.

In 1999, Howard became the first Black woman ever to command a US Navy warship. Ten years later, she was the first African-American woman to lead a Navy battle group. Her negotiations with Somali pirates who had taken her captain hostage was depicted in the film Captain Phillips.

Howard continued to rise through the Navy's ranks, eventually becoming the first woman ever to be promoted to four-star General. At the same time, Howard became vice chief of the US's naval operations - the 2nd highest ranking position in the whole Navy.

In 2020, Howard was appointed by President-Elect Joe Biden to serve on his transition team for the Department of Defense.

1960-

judith jamison
dancer - choreographer - director

Judith Jamison started dancing when she was 6 years, and she kept on dancing in the US and internationally for almost twenty years.

In 1989 she became the artistic director for the Alvin Ailey American Dance Theater, where she had once been a star performer.

The Ailey Theater had been founded to give Black dancers more opportunities to perform pieces about African-American experiences and culture. Jamison furthered this mission even as she brought in new performers and her own style as a choreographer.

Jamison breathed new life into the center's educational mission, dramatically improved its finances, and oversaw the building of the Theater's first permanent home. Jamison's autobiography, Dancing Spirit, was published in 1993.

1943-

mae jemison
astronaut - physician

Mae Jemison is the first Black woman ever to become an astronaut in the National Aeronautics and Space Administration (NASA).

As a child and young adult, Jemison had many different interests besides science. She got dual degrees in engineering and Afro-American studies and then went on to become a doctor.

She provided medical services in Africa for the Peace Corps before joining NASA.

Jemison was chosen from among almost 2,000 candidates to become an astronaut.

She became the first Black woman in space when she served as mission specialist for the space shuttle Endeavour.

Her job included performing spacewalks and doing experiments from orbit.

After she left NASA, Jemison founded an educational non-profit, wrote children's books, and made TV appearances.

Jemison has been inducted into the International Space Hall of Fame and the Women's Hall of Fame.

1956-

beverly johnson
model - actor - businessperson

At age 21, fashion model Beverly Johnson became the first African-American woman ever to appear on the cover of Vogue magazine.

Within a few years, she was one of the best-paid supermodels in the industry.

Johnson's appeal was long-lasting - she continued modeling into her 40s. She was featured on about 500 magazine covers overall.

The daughter of a Louisiana Creole mother and a Blackfoot American Indian father, Johnson was an athlete in her youth and almost qualified for freestyle swimming at the Olympics.

After she left modeling, Johnson starred in some TV roles, created her own line of wigs and hair products for Black women, and wrote books on beauty and health. She starred in her own reality TV series on the OWN Network in 2012.

1952-

kellie jones
art historian - curator

Kellie Jones has spent her career bringing attention to Black artists from the present and past whose work has been ignored or excluded by mainstream society.

Jones has done much especially to organize international exhibits of important Black artists from the 1960s and 1970s. She wants to create a more inclusive history of art.

Jones grew up in New York City. Her parents were both creative writers, and their circle of artistic friends was diverse. When Jones studied the history of art in college, in contrast, she found that it focused mostly on white - or dead - artists.

She decided that becoming a curator and academic would give her the chance to introduce unknown artists of color to the world, ones living as well as dead, and her path was set.

Jones' work fighting for the recognition of neglected Black art and artists was rewarded in 2016 when the MacArthur Foundation awarded her a Genius Grant of $625,000.

1959-

leslie jones
comedian - actor

It took more than two decades on the road performing at comedy clubs for Leslie Jones to become a breakout star.

She found a famous champion in Chris Rock, who cast her in a film and then suggested her for consideration by the TV show Saturday Night Live (SNL).

Jones was hired in 2014 as a writer for SNL but soon became a performer on it.

Soon, she was appearing in magazines and TV commercials and being interviewed on talk shows. Another big break came when she was cast in the feature film Ghostbusters.

A former high school and college basketball player who stands more than 6 feet tall, Jones specializes in physical, outspoken comedy.

Jones remembers crying as a girl when she saw Whoopi Goldberg performing on TV. Jones had never seen people on TV who looked like her before then.

Seeing Goldberg made Jones realize that she, too, could be on TV.

1967-

jackie joyner-kersee
athlete

Jackie Joyner-Kersee is one of the most incredible American track athletes of all time.

The winner of three Olympic gold medals, one silver, and one bronze, Joyner-Kersee set a world record in the Olympic heptathlon, a series of seven track events. And she was the first American in history to win a gold medal in the long jump.

Before Joyner-Kersee won the heptathlon, few people in America really noticed it, but after her record-setting win, it became one of the most popular Olympic events. Participants earn points by competing in high and long jumps, 100-meter hurdles, shot put, javelin throwing, a 200-meter dash, and an 800-meter run.

As a girl, Joyner-Kersee grew up in poverty in Illinois. Her parents were very young - her mother only 16 when she gave birth to Jackie two years after having a son, Al. Joyner-Kersee was named after Jacqueline Kennedy-Onassis in the hopes that she would go on to great things.

Joyner-Kersee and her brother Al became very close, inspiring and competing against one another.

Both of them went on to become Olympic gold medalists.

1962-

alicia keys
singer - songwriter - producer

Alicia Keys' triple-platinum first album, Songs in A Minor, made her a breakout star, and for good reason. Not only did she sing beautifully, but she also co-produced, wrote most of her own lyrics and music, and played the instruments. It was no surprise when the album won five Grammy awards.

Keys is the daughter of an African-American father and Italian-American mother. She was raised mostly by her mother, whose earnings were not enough to avoid financial struggles.

But Keys' mother fostered her daughter's love of music no matter the cost, insisting on paying for piano lessons.

Keys worked tirelessly on her voice, song-writing, and playing as a child and as a high school student at the Professional Performance Arts School in Manhattan where she had earned a place.

Keys graduated high school at age 16 and was accepted into Columbia University. A record deal with Columbia Records led her to walk away from college. Even though that deal fell through, Keys eventually recorded her first album, and the rest is history.

1981-

henrietta lacks

medical research subject

Completely unknown to her, Henrietta Lacks made possible incredible medical breakthroughs.

In 1951, while she was being treated for cervical cancer at Johns Hopkins Hospital, Lacks' doctors harvested some of her cancer cells. It turned out that these cells, named HeLa cells after Lacks, were the first human cells that could live in a laboratory for an indefinite period of time. Other cells always died after reproducing only a few times.

Without Lacks' or her family's knowledge or consent, her cells were mass produced and distributed to laboratories that were doing research of various kinds.

Lacks' HeLa cells were vital to the development of the 1952 polio vaccine and a score of later advances in areas like in vitro fertilization, chemotherapy, and gene mapping.

Despite radiation treatments, Lacks died from cervical cancer in 1951. Her story only became well-known when Rebecca Skloot uncovered the truth in her best-selling 2010 book, The Immortal Life of Henrietta Lacks.

1920–1951

lizzo
hip-hop artist

Lizzo, born Melissa Jefferson, has taken the world by storm with her positive messages encouraging people, especially women, to accept and love themselves and to take charge of their own lives.

Lizzo's love of music began in her hometown of Detroit, where she grew up listening to gospel songs in her religious household. After the family moved to Houston when she was 10, Lizzo began playing the flute.

She joined her first band while in Houston. When she and her mother moved to Minneapolis, with its quirky music scene, Lizzo says she figured out how to fuse her love of rap, gospel, and indie music.

It took a lot of work, and several albums, before Lizzo broke out. Her album Big GRRRL Small World brought Lizzo viral attention for its upbeat messages encouraging women to love themselves and their bodies, no matter the size. Her third studio album in 2019 gained mainstream acceptance, nearing the top of the Billboard 500 list.

Lizzo was nominated for 8 Grammy Awards - the most of any performer that year - and won three. Time magazine named her Entertainer of the Year.

1988-

mildred loving
homemaker, civil rights activist

Mildred Loving didn't set out to be a hero. But when the State of Virginia tried to prevent her from marrying the man she loved, she became one.

Born of African-American and Native American heritage, Loving grew up in a rural area where many mixed-race people lived. And so it was not seen as unusual when she and her white friend from childhood, Richard Loving, became a couple.

But when Mildred Loving became pregnant and the pair decided to marry, they came face-to-face with the Virginia law that made it illegal for people of different races to marry.

To get around this, the couple drove to Washington, DC, which had no such law, married, and went back to Virginia.

One night at about 2 am, Loving awoke to find a policeman by her bed, and she and her husband were arrested and charged.

The two moved to Washington DC but were again arrested in Virginia when they came to visit their families.

Eventually, the Lovings enlisted the help of an attorney who took their case all the way to the Supreme Court. The Supreme Court voted unanimously that the Virginia law - and all others like it - was unconstitutional.

1939-2008

toni morrison
writer

Toni Morrison was one of the most celebrated American writers of all time. Not only did she win the Pulitzer Prize for her novel Beloved, but in 1993 she became the first Black woman ever to win the Nobel Prize for Literature.

Her novels focus on the struggles of Black characters to rediscover and stay connected to their history and ancestors.

Morrison's commitment to helping the Black community remember and honor its past and its folklore extended into her college teaching and editorial occupations.

As a senioreditor for Random House, Morrison published other Black writers with important stories to tell, including Angela Davis and Gayl Jones.

In 1974, Morrison edited The Black Book, which was a collection of newspaper clippings, advertisements, photographs, and other artifacts left behind over 300 years of Black history.

About the book, Morrison wrote that she hoped it would help Blacks to "recognize and rescue those qualities of resistance, excellence, and integrity that were so much a part of our past and so useful to us and the generations of blacks now growing up."

1931-2019

thandi newton
actor

Thandi Newton is the daughter of a Zimbabwean mother and English father. Her family left Africa for England when she was five years old to escape political unrest.

Newton says she sees her mixed-race heritage as a strength, and herself as a bridge between the races. Her dark skin and refined English accent often take people in the movie industry by surprise, she says, challenging their racial assumptions.

In her film and TV roles, Newton has played a range of roles - from a slave in the film adaptation of Toni Morrison's Beloved to the female lead in a blockbuster action movie co-starring Tom Cruise.

Beginning in 2016, Newton took on the role of the strong, self-aware female android Maeve in HBO's series Westworld. She has won a Primetime Emmy Award for Outstanding Supporting Actress in a Drama Series and two Critics Choice Awards for her performance in the series.

1972-

michelle obama
author, lawyer

For eight years, Michelle Obama was best known as President Barack Obama's First Lady and as a self-described "mom-in-chief" of daughters Sasha and Malia.

But Obama is much more. Born in a modest neighborhood in Chicago's South Shore, she was a gifted student. She skipped second grade, was in her high school's honors program, and went on to Princeton University and Harvard Law School.

After earning her law degree, she went to work as a corporate attorney in Chicago, where she met her future husband.

Dissatisfied with her work, Obama left for a career in public service, beginning in the Chicago Mayor's office and then holding a succession of roles helping young adults find public service opportunities and prepare for careers in public service. She also performed broader community outreach and promoted diversity and minority hires.

When her husband decided to run for President, Obama showed herself a confident and effective public speaker. As First Lady, she led an initiative against childhood obesity.

Obama's 2018 memoir, Becoming, sold over 10 million copies the year it was released, and she had a wildly successful book tour. In 2020, she launched The Michelle Obama Podcast.

1964-

lorraine o'grady
artist, writer

Lorraine O'Grady is a performance and photo artist whose works comment forcefully on American racial and gender issues.

O'Grady is the daughter of well-off Jamaican parents of mixed Caribbean, African and Irish heritage. Living in Boston, O'Grady saw early on that her life of privilege was very different from most of the lives lived in Boston's African-American and Irish communities.

She lacked a clear focus in her twenties and thirties, switching majors, marrying, divorcing, having a child, and marrying again. She moved around as she worked as an economist, rock and roll critic, and translator. At long last she discovered the visual arts, where she found her calling. The African-American art that she saw lacked boldness, in her view, and she set out to shake up the art world.

In her first performance art installation, O'Grady wore a fancy dress and tiara and chanted, 'THAT'S ENOUGH - No more boot licking ... BLACK ART MUST TAKE MORE RISKS!'

Many of her works are feminist and criticize the ways that Black women are represented in American culture. O'Grady has received numerous grants that help support her daring work.

1934-

na'taki osborne
environmental scientist and activist

Na'taki Osborne grew up in Baton Rouge, Louisiana, near 'Cancer Alley' - 85 miles along the Mississippi River heavily polluted by industrial plants. Even the water and air smelled and tasted bad.

When her mother was diagnosed with breast cancer, Osborne knew she had to do something. At college, she majored in in engineering and chemistry and went to intern with the Environmental Protection Agency (EPA). For her internship, Osborne volunteered to work in the Carver Hills neighborhood in Atlanta.

She organized 300 volunteers to help clean up the filthy creek running through the area and did educational outreach with the neighborhood children, teaching them how to make homemade water filters and to monitor the quality of the water in the creek.

Osborne's work was so impressive that leaders of the EPA came to Atlanta to see her in action.

Then and in the years since, Osborne has been a tireless environmental activist and community leader who has encouraged grass roots fights for environmental justice.

1974-

marjorie b. parham
editor - publisher

When Marjorie B. Parham was in high school, there were few careers considered suitable for women, but Parham had no intention of becoming a teacher, nurse or social worker.

Parham attended Wilberforce University, a historically Black college in Ohio. After a short-lived first marriage produced a son, she took a job as a clerk in the Veterans Administration in Cincinnati.

But it was her second marriage that would set Parham's career path. Her second husband, Gerald Porter, founded a weekly newspaper called the Cincinnati Herald, which was aimed at the city's African-American community, and the Dayton Tribune.

When her son was drafted, Parham took over the Dayton Tribune, despite having no experience in journalism.

Two years later, her husband was involved in a car accident, but the hospital where he was taken refused to treat him because he was Black. Her husband died.

Parham shut down the Dayton paper and took over the Herald, which she personally ran for nearly 30 years.

In 2020, Cincinnati renamed one of its streets Marjorie Parham Way to honor her 102nd birthday.

1918-

rosa parks
civil rights activist

On December 1, 1955, Rosa Parks broke the law when she refused to give up her seat on a city bus in Montgomery, Alabama, to a white man. Parks was tired - not just from a day's work but of a lifetime lived under the Jim Crow laws of the American South. She was sick of drinking from Blacks-only water fountains and of missing lunch because whites-only restaurants wouldn't serve her.

Parks' act of defiance sparked a revolution that one day would help Black Americans achieve equal treatment under the law. In Montgomery, most people who rode the bus were Black, but the four front seats were reserved for whites. The middle section of the bus could be used by Black riders only if no whites needed seats. This unjust law infuriated Parks, and she often walked home to avoid riding the bus at all.

The day she made history, a white man got on the bus and demanded the middle seats be cleared out. Parks refused to move. The bus driver called the police, and Parks was taken to the police station, finger-printed, booked, and locked up. Eventually she paid a fine of $10 plus $4 in court costs.

For more than a year afterward, almost the entire Black community in Montgomery boycotted the buses in support of her - as the world watched. The Supreme Court finally ruled against segregation on Montgomery public transportation in 1956. Eight more years would have to pass, though, before the Civil Rights Act of 1964 made public transportation segregation illegal nationally.

1913-2005

condoleeza rice
secretary of state - national security advisor

Condoleezza Rice's parents instilled in her an interest in both politics and piano playing. In college, Rice first majored in piano performance but then switched to political science, graduating with highest honors at the age of 19. She went on to earn a doctorate in international studies and taught political science at Stanford University. Rice soon became known for her expertise in US-Soviet Union affairs and became an adviser to the US Joint Chiefs of Staff and Air Force.

In 1989, Rice was appointed director of Soviet and East European affairs on the National Security Council. Her role was to analyze the events going on in these areas for President George H. W. Bush. Rice prepared the President for important summit meetings with the Soviet president and other international officials. The purpose of these meetings was to work on creating a global plan for peace.

After her service to the President, Rice returned to academia for a time, but in 2000 she returned to the White House as George W. Bush's National Security Advisor - the first African-American and first woman ever to hold the position.

After the September 11, 2001, attacks and the start of the Iraqi War, Rice became a leading spokesperson for Bush's foreign policy. Eventually Bush named Rice to succeed General Colin Powell as Secretary of State, a position she held to the end of Bush's administration.

1954-

amelia boynton robinson
civil rights activist

Amelia Boyton Robinson was known as 'Queen Mother' because of her exceptional leadership early in the voting rights movement. African-American voters in Alabama (like other areas of the American South) were intentionally prevented from voting by unfair literacy and other tests.

Robinson and her husband became the leaders of the voting rights movement in Selma, Alabama. Robinson was mistreated by police repeatedly when she led voter drives and protests in Selma.

She became famous for a day that came to be known as Bloody Sunday. She and other organizers planned a 50-mile march of 600 activists to protest the suppression of Black voters. They intended to cross the Edmund Pettus Bridge leading from Selma to Montgomery, the capital of Alabama.

Nearly 200 state troopers, along with posses of deputized white men, sprayed fire hoses on the protesters and set dogs on them to stop their march. The protesters were gassed and beaten. A photo of Robinson, clubbed by a white officer and lying unconscious beneath him on the ground, made the activist famous - while drawing nationwide attention to the voting rights movement.

Robinson remained active in the civil rights movement for the rest of her life. Shortly before her death at age 104, Robinson, in a wheelchair, crossed the Edmund Pettus Bridge hand-in-hand with President Barack Obama to commemorate the 50th anniversary of Bloody Sunday.

1911-2015

amy sherald
painter

Amy Sherald is best-known for the life-sized portrait of Michelle Obama that she painted at the First Lady's request. But her path to artistic fame and success was not an easy one.

Sherald's parents wanted her to go into medicine, but she knew as a child that path wasn't one she wanted to take. When her school class went on a museum field trip and Sherald saw her first painting of a Black person, she knew what her career would be. She would be an artist.

She studied for a BA and MFA in painting, learning and improving her craft by working under other painters in the United States and abroad. Her career was interrupted at age 30 when she was diagnosed with congestive heart failure. Nine years later, Sherald received a heart transplant, and she was able to return to painting with enthusiasm.

In 2016, Sherald became the first Black woman ever to win the Outwin Boochever Portrait Competition for the National Portrait Gallery in Washington, DC. In 2017, First Lady Michelle Obama chose Sherald to paint her official portrait. One of the defining features of Sherald's art is her use of grisaille (tones of gray) rather than natural Black skin tones. Sherald's goal is to remove visible traces of race from the painting so that the person depicted is the focus of the art.

1973-

margaret simms
economist

Economist Margaret Simms came of age as segregation was ending. Until fifth grade, she attended segregated schools in St. Louis, Missouri.

When she attended college in Minnesota, there were only four African-Americans in the student body of 1,400. She went on to study for a masters degree and Ph.D. at Stanford University in a program where only one Black person - and no women - had earned their doctorate.

During Simms' first year at Stanford, Martin Luther King, Jr. was assassinated. Simms chose to focus on urban economics so she could work to improve people's understanding of inequality and to increase opportunity.

Simms has gone on to become one of the leading experts on economic issues affecting Black Americans. She has worked as director of the Urban Institute's Minorities and Social Policy Program and - later - as its director of the Low-Income Working Families project.

Among her publications are two volumes of policy that she co-edited, Slipping through the Cracks: The Status of Black Women and The Economics of Race and Crime.

1946-

norma merrick sklarek
architect

Before Norma Merrick Sklarek, no Black woman had ever been a licensed architect in the US. All that changed in 1954 when Sklarek passed the New York State architect examination. Over the next three decades, Sklarek designed many impressive projects, including Terminal 1 at Los Angeles International Airport and the American Embassy in Tokyo.

Sklarek was born in Harlem, but her parents moved to Brooklyn when she was a child. With academic strengths and interests in math, science, and the arts, Sklarek wasn't sure what to she wanted to study in college. Her father recommended architecture, which combined all of these interests.

Sklarek knew nothing about the field of architecture. Few African-Americans worked in the profession. She took a leap of faith and won a spot in Cornell University's competitive architecture program. After graduation, she passed the challenging four-day state architecture exam and became the first Black woman ever licensed as an architect.

Sklarek worked at prestigious architectural design firms in New York and Los Angeles before going on to found and co-found her own firms. One of the firms designed the Bellagio Hotel in Las Vegas, while Sklarek herself designed several high-profile public buildings.

1928-2012

angie thomas
author

Angie Thomas became a breakout novelist with her young adult novel, The Hate U Give, which sold 100,000 copies in its first month. Inspired by Black Lives Matter, the book opened up an important discussion in America about racism, social injustice, and police violence. The book tells the story of a Black girl named Starr Carter, who witnesses the shooting of her friend by a white police officer and becomes an activist.

Thomas grew up poor in Jackson, Mississippi, where she was no stranger to gun violence. The six-year-old Thomas was at a park when drug dealers started firing at each other. Thomas ran away so she wouldn't be hurt. The next day, her mother took her to the library to show her there were other worlds out there. Although Thomas loved stories, she hated that the books didn't represent people like her.

In college, her professor encouraged her to write stories drawn from her experiences and her community. Thomas was inspired to write by the fatal police shooting of the unarmed Black 22-year old Oscar Grant in California. Thomas was angered by the killing - and by hearing white students at her university say that Grant 'deserved it.'

Eventually Thomas' story became The Hate U Give. The book debuted at #1 on the New York Times young adult best-seller list. Thomas's second young adult novel, On the Come Up, was published in 2019.

1988-

beauty turner
journalist - activist - entrepreneur

Beauty Turner was a single mother who raised three children in one of the worst public housing projects in Chicago's South Side, Robert Taylor. What she saw and lived there inspired her to become an activist for Chicago's poor and neglected people.

Living in the Robert Taylor project, Turner saw how helpless the residents were in getting the city's help with crime, leaks, pest infestations and the like. She decided to become a journalist to publicize conditions at the project and studied for years to find the right resources. Then she wrote editorials and human interest stories and managed some small victories with the city.

The project was eventually torn down, and its residents relocated. Turner then started Beauty's Ghetto Bus Tours to make Chicago's forgotten neighborhoods visible and to start conversations between the City's visitors and its public housing residents.

1957-2008

dorothy vaughn

mathematician - computer programmer

Dorothy Vaughn worked for the US Government during World War II in an all-Black group of female mathematicians and computer programmers. The women worked to support research and development in US air warfare.

From a young age, Vaughn had a talent for math. Under a full scholarship to the country's first historically Black college, Wilberforce University in Ohio, Vaughan majored in math, but because of the financial pressures of the Great Depression on her family, finished her degree in education with a mathematics major.

In 1943, she responded to a job advertisement for mathematicians with the federal government and soon joined the group of all-Black female 'computers,' as they were called. After the war ended, Vaughn stayed on and became the first Black supervisor ever for her unit, the West End Computing Unit. The unit by then had been made a part of NASA, as the US was beginning its new space program.

Her story - and her fellow workers' - is told in the nonfiction book Hidden Figures: The American Dream and the Untold Story of the Black Women Mathematicians Who Helped Win the Space Race.

1910-2008

renita weems
theologian - educator - writer

Theologian Renita Weems took a roundabout route through her faith and career.

Her religious upbringing and her mother's abandonment of the family deeply affected her.

Although initially she completed an economics degree and worked as a stockbroker, Weems abandoned that path to become a freelance writer and to study theology.

In 1979 Weems was ordained as a minister in the African Methodist Episcopal Church. Then she completed masters and doctoral degrees in divinity at Princeton University. She was the first Black woman ever to earn a Ph. D. in Old Testament Studies at the University.

She did not choose a life in the ministry because of the bias against women at the time. Female ministers were ridiculed by male ministers and were given only the most undesirable assignments.

Weems believed she could reach far more people through a career in academia and through her writing. She has written spiritual memoirs and analyses of the Old Testament. She also co-authored gospel star CeCe Winans' spiritual autobiography.

Every year, Weems runs a spiritual retreat called Just a Sister Away. She also manages Somethingwithin.com: An E-Journal for Women Seeking Balance.

1954-

venus williams
tennis player

Venus Williams, like her mega-talented younger sister Serena, has taken the game of tennis by storm.

By age 10, Venus Williams had a winning streak of 63 games and had won the Southern California under-12 title. Sports Illustrated and Tennis magazine both ran stories on her. She was accepted into a prestigious Florida tennis academy, and the whole family relocated so she could enroll.

Williams took a break from competing for four years while she trained six days a week, six hours a day, and home-schooled. By the time Williams turned 13, companies were already offering her endorsement deals in anticipation of her going pro.

At age 14, she did just that, but it would take a while for her to readjust to competition. In 2000, Williams won the singles title at Wimbledon - the first African-American to do so since Althea Gibson in 1958. She has had so many more wins since then that it's hard to keep up with her - at Wimbledon, the US Open, the Olympics, and elsewhere.

Williams has become a celebrity in other ways, too, publishing a book, designing clothing, and starring in a reality-TV show.

1980-

oprah winfrey
media executive, talk show host, actress

One of the most influential Americans in history, billionaire Oprah Winfrey has created a multimedia empire.

In 1986, Winfrey became the first nationally-syndicated talk show host who was both Black and a woman. Winfrey's talents as a host led her to be called 'The Queen of Talk.'

On her show, Winfrey was honest about her struggles to lose weight and history of abuse.

At the core of Winfrey's message then and now is the importance of helping others - not only for its own sake but to enhance personal well-being. Winfrey is one of the top Black philanthropists in the country.

She fought especially hard for the passage of the 1993 National Child Protection Act, also called 'The Oprah Bill,' which requires strict sentences for child abusers. The bill was signed into law by President Bill Clinton.

Besides hosting her own show for 25 years, Winfrey has started her own production company and TV network, taken on acting roles, and published her own magazine.

Winfrey has received numerous honors for her work as an entertainer and philanthropist.

1954-